SandCastle
Tools of the Trade

PLIERS

ANDERS HANSON

Consulting Editor, Diane Craig, M.A./Reading Specialist

ABDO
Publishing Company

Published by ABDO Publishing Company, 8000 West 78th Street, Edina, Minnesota 55439.

Copyright © 2010 by Abdo Consulting Group, Inc. International copyrights reserved in all countries.

Printed in the United States.

Editor: Pam Price
Content Developer: Nancy Tuminelly
Cover and Interior Design and Production: Mighty Media
Photo Credits: Shutterstock, iStockphoto (Lauri Wiberg, Jason Lugo, Rich Legg)

Library of Congress Cataloging-in-Publication Data
Hanson, Anders, 1980-
  Pliers / Anders Hanson.
    p. cm. -- (Tools of the trade)
  ISBN 978-1-60453-583-9
  1. Pliers--Juvenile literature. I. Title.

TJ1201.T65H35 2009
621.9'92--dc22
                            2008055714

SandCastle™ Level: Fluent

SandCastle™ books are created by a team of professional educators, reading specialists, and content developers around five essential components—phonemic awareness, phonics, vocabulary, text comprehension, and fluency—to assist young readers as they develop reading skills and strategies and increase their general knowledge. All books are written, reviewed, and leveled for guided reading, early reading intervention, and Accelerated Reader® programs for use in shared, guided, and independent reading and writing activities to support a balanced approach to literacy instruction. The SandCastle™ series has four levels that correspond to early literacy development. The levels are provided to help teachers and parents select appropriate books for young readers.

Emerging Readers
(no flags)

Beginning Readers
(1 flag)

Transitional Readers
(2 flags)

Fluent Readers
(3 flags)

SandCastle™ would like to hear from you. Please send us your comments and suggestions.
sandcastle@abdopublishing.com

CONTENTS

locking pliers

WHAT ARE PLIERS?

handles

jaws

Pliers are tools that grip and bend objects. Some pliers can cut things too. Pliers have handles that open and close like a pair of scissors. The head of the pliers has jaws that grip things.

HISTORY

No one knows who invented the first pliers. The earliest pliers were probably made of sticks and used to move hot coals.

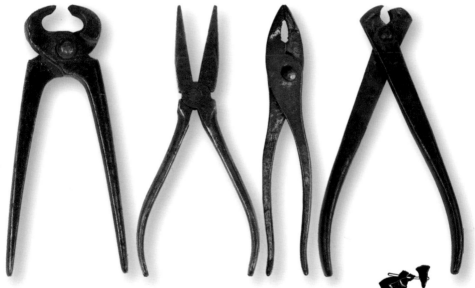

By 2000 BC, **blacksmiths** were using pliers to work with hot metals.

ancient Egyptian blacksmith

SLIP-JOINT PLIERS

Slip-joint pliers often have two sets of teeth. One set is fine, and the other is **coarse**. The fine teeth grip small things such as nails. The coarse teeth grip larger objects such as nuts or bolts.

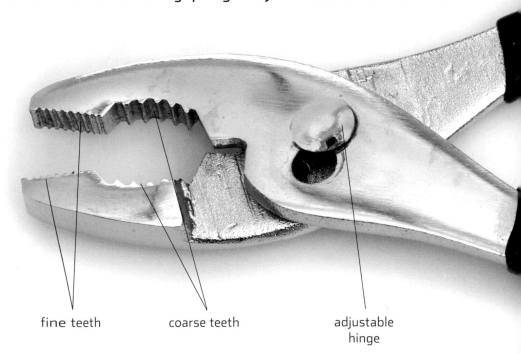

fine teeth   coarse teeth   adjustable hinge

Slip-joint pliers have an **adjustable hinge** so the jaws can move farther apart.

handle

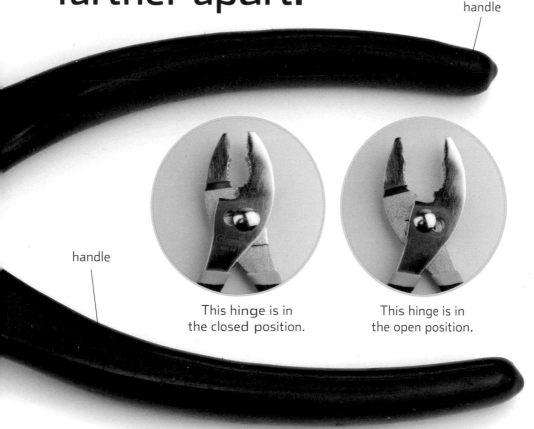

handle

This hinge is in the closed position.

This hinge is in the open position.

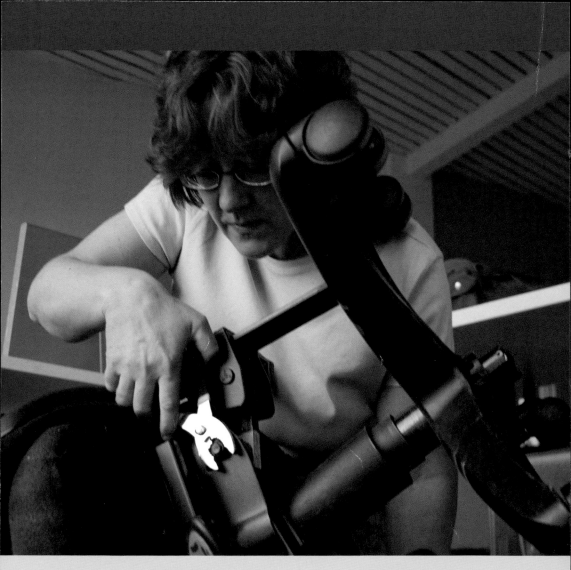

Candice is fixing a chair. She tightens
a nut with slip-joint pliers.

Jaime is hooking up cable television.
He uses slip-joint pliers to attach the cable.

LINEMAN'S PLIERS

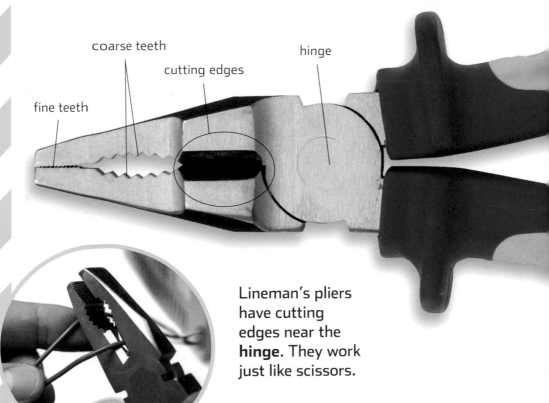

fine teeth

coarse teeth

cutting edges

hinge

Lineman's pliers have cutting edges near the **hinge.** They work just like scissors.

Lineman's pliers grip, bend, and cut objects such as wire and cable.

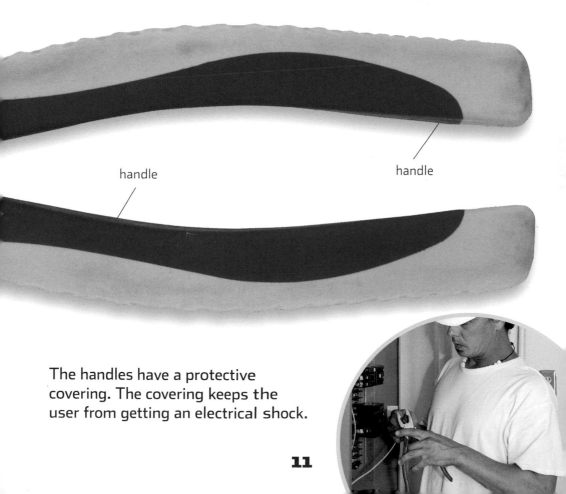

handle

handle

The handles have a protective covering. The covering keeps the user from getting an electrical shock.

Mark is an electrician. He uses lineman's pliers to cut and strip wires.

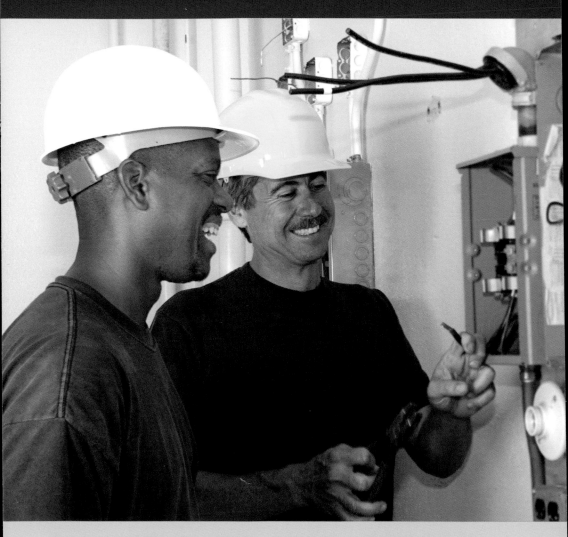

Paul and Matt use lineman's pliers while working with electrical wires.

LOCKING PLIERS

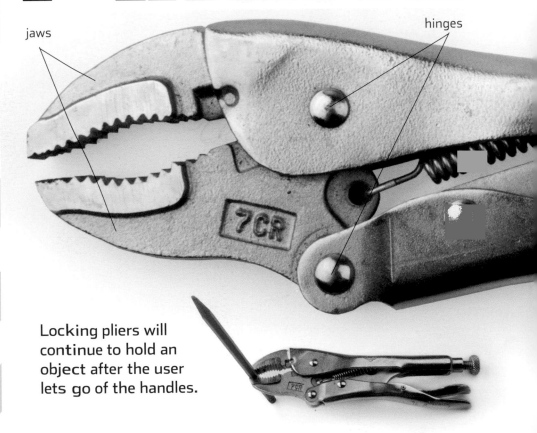

jaws

hinges

7CR

Locking pliers will
continue to hold an
object after the user
lets go of the handles.

The jaws of locking pliers can be locked in place.

Turn the **adjusting** bolt to open or close the jaws. Then squeeze the handles to lock the jaws.

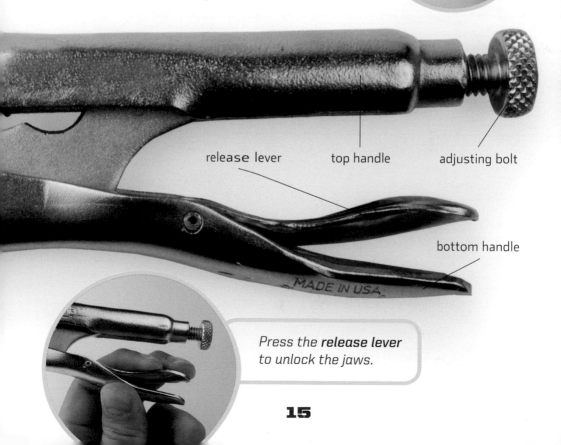

release lever

top handle

adjusting bolt

bottom handle

MADE IN USA

Press the *release lever* to unlock the jaws.

Ron is **welding**. He uses locking pliers to hold the metal pieces.

Becky is fixing a leaky sink. Locking pliers help her tighten the pipe fittings.

NEEDLE-NOSE PLIERS

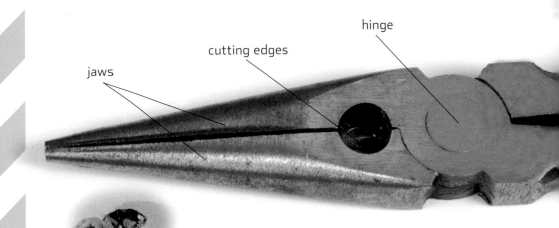

hinge

cutting edges

jaws

Needle-nose pliers are often used by electricians and **hobbyists.**

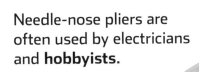

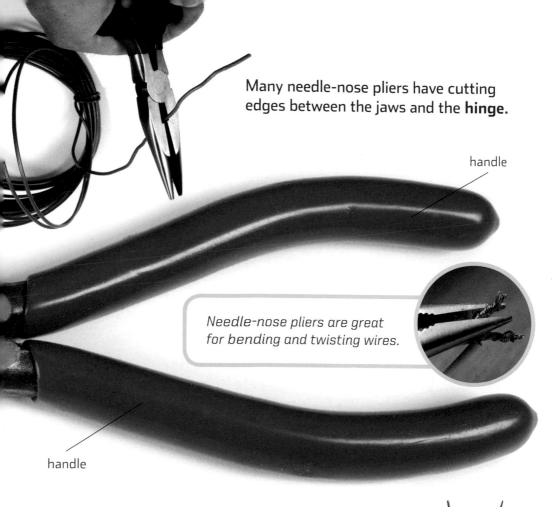

Many needle-nose pliers have cutting edges between the jaws and the **hinge**.

handle

Needle-nose pliers are great for bending and twisting wires.

handle

Needle-nose pliers have long, thin jaws.

The narrow jaws can reach into small spaces.

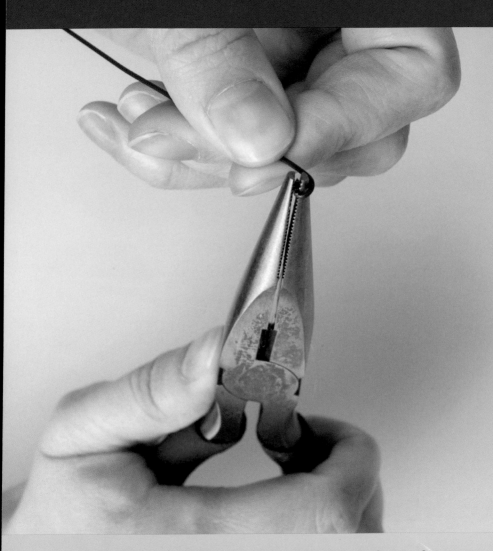

Erin uses needle-nose pliers to bend a wire.
She is working on a craft project.

Emily is making a necklace.
She uses needle-nose pliers to grip a wire.

MATCH GAME

Match the words to the pictures! The answers are on the bottom of the page.

1. locking pliers

A.

2. needle-nose pliers

B.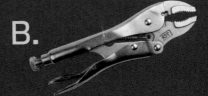

3. slip-joint pliers

C.

4. lineman's pliers

D.

TOOL QUIZ

Test your tool knowledge with this quiz!
The answers are on the bottom of the page.

1. Slip-joint pliers do not have a hinge. True or false?

2. Lineman's pliers have cutting edges. True or false?

3. The jaws of locking pliers can be locked. True or false?

4. Needle-nose pliers have short, thick jaws. True or false?

Answers: 1) false 2) true 3) true 4) false

GLOSSARY

adjust – to change something slightly to produce a desired result. An object is *adjustable* if it is designed to be used in more than one way.

blacksmith – a person who works with iron.

coarse – made for less-delicate work.

hinge – a joint that allows two attached parts to move.

hobbyist – a person who does an activity for fun and relaxation.

lever – a handle used to control or operate a device.

release – to set free or let go.

weld – to join metal parts by heating the metal until the parts flow together.